AWS:

2019 Complete Guide for Beginner's. Amazon Web Services Tutorial.

AWS

ISBN: 9781686808067

CONTENTS

Thank you for purchasing this book!

We always try to give more value then you expect. That's why we've updated the content and you can get it for FREE. You can get the digital version for free because you bought the print version.

The book is under the match program from Amazon. You can find how to do this using next URL: https://www.amazon.com/gp/digital/ep-landing-page

I hope it will be useful for you.

Introduction

Amazon Web Services is a great way to build your programs through the Amazon portal. With Amazon Web Services, you can

do a lot with this, and there are a lot of great things you can do. In addition, it is also incredibly cheap compared to other developer services. But, what is so special about it? What can you do with it?

Well, you are about to find out. In this, we will give you a beginner's look at Amazon web services, and what it can do for you. We will also tell you how to launch websites, how to register domain names, and even services for big data and services for coding as well.

The beauty of AWS is that it can be used to create so many different elements to this, and you will be able to create and craft some wonderful codes and programs for your company. Hosting some of these can get expensive, but AWS makes it super easy for you to do, and we will tell you about what it is, the benefits of this, and what you can get from this too. That way, you will be able to do so much more with it, and you can start building your business and life in so many different ways. If you've been interested in AWS in the past, but you don't really know how to get started with this, then you'll definitely want to keep on reading about this, since there is so much you can do with this, and a lot that can help you build a much better and more reasonable action that will make your life easier, and allow you to code some of the important elements that you want to code.

Chapter 1 – What is AWS?

When it comes to AWS, you may wonder what it is, and you may be curious about some of the different aspects of this. Well, you are in luck, because there is a lot you can do with it, and here, we will tell you how to get started with AWS, and build the business that you love.

So What is It?

To put it simply, AWS, or Amazon Web Services is a secure platform with cloud services, which allows you to compute various actions, store data, deliver content, and also other functions that help businesses grow and scale as well. You can run applications and host websites, store your files directly to the cloud, manage data bases that are SQL, and also deliver files both static and dynamic to various areas. If you're someone who is dealing with email marketing as well, you can even send bulk emails to your customers!

AWS has a lot of services, and over 165 different servers, and 40 that are only available to Amazon. It has the largest community of both partners and customers, and it is super secure, very good for operational expertise, and it actually was only released about a year ago. So, it's certainly matched up to a lot of the needs that people have.

AWS currently is available in as many as 66 different zones, and 21 different geographic regions within the world, and in a bunch of regions in locations such as Jakarta and Milan. So, it's growing. With the way Amazon has started to push forward into being a global powerhouse, it's no wonder why people aren't turning to other security instruments.

Why Use It?

AWS has been around since 2004, but in the last year, it has been made into a whole new powerhouse. Businesses can use this these days to create a great IT infrastructure including servers, well in advance. You can get results by accessing a bunch of virtual servers. This means, you do not have to pay a lot for the security that you're getting.

It is also incredibly secure. The web services creates a means for you to have durable, along with secure technology on your platform. Amazon data centers have layers of security, and AWS always audit their structures for pure security. It is great because it also has a lot of security features, and it makes sure that everything is confidential, and it also has "end to end" privacy along with security too.

This also does not have any extra expenses, and it's literally just "pay as you go" which means that you're saving a ton of money, and allowing for a much stronger global infrastructure. You do not need to invest in any commodities, you will also have more secure, and better customer satisfaction with this too, and you'll be able to maximize your ROI.

Finally, ti's incredibly flexible. Whether you're computing, or migrating legacy apps to the cloud, or whatever, you don't have to rewrite anything, but instead, you just put it on there, and AWS helps you create a productive ecosystem as well.

With AWS becoming the source for many people to look into for their cloud computing needs, it's no wonder why people are choosing this over other structures, and you'll be amazed by the nature, and what you can do with this.

Chapter 2 – Getting Started with AWS

So you've learned what it is, but do you know how to begin with AWS? Well, you're in luck, for here, we'll tell you a bit about how you can get started with AWS, and where you begin with this service so you can net some wonderful results.

Begin with Your Server

To begin, you need to first and foremost, sign up with AWS, and you'll need a server, which is called the Elastic Compute Cloud, or EC2, so you can click on that from the home console, and from there launch instance to set up the virtual server. You then want to choose the Ubuntu server, if you're using Ubuntu for example.

Next, you've got to choose your instance, whether it be with more powerful CPUs, or if you're starting with a small project. The t2.micro is the best option for this, and once you start to get users, you can upgrade to bigger. Plus, it's free for the first year. From there, you configure the security group, which is the next step to make a change towards.

AWS is about security and scalability, and most instances have security groups that determine where the traffic is going. If you don't want your server to be compromised by the internet, you should create a security group. You will want to make sure that you can put the traffic to port 22, and from there, over to the HTTP which is port 80, or the HTTPS which is port 443, and once that's there, you can continue on.

From there, you launch it, and you'll want to from there, download private key files, which is used to connect to your server with the SSH. It can usually be called whatever. From there, you finally want to click the launch instance option.

You can from there check everything out, and from there, you'll then be able to see the state of the server, and proceed with connecting to it.

Connecting to the Instance

Once you've launched the instance., now you will want to connect to it. Essentially you connect it and use it in the computer, and to do this, you select your EC2 instance. You're using, and then connect. You should from there, you should select the Java SSH client from the browser. Remember that private key path/ well, now you should do that, and from there, you can launch the SSH client. That means, you're connected!

Now, you can also see the public IP for the server. Chances are, if you get an error, you didn't change the permissions, and that means that you need to put in chmod 400, memegen.pem in order to make this work.

Now finally, if you need to set up the secure server, you'll want to run the NodeJS, and from there, you should see a directory there, and you can install it, and then install Express, and then create an index file. At this point, you should then see the "hello world" text when you go to the server roots.

And there you have it! you'll then be able to begin with AWS, and as you can see, it's definitely not as complex as you think it is.

Chapter 3 – Development Services for Website Owners

Web developers will enjoy all of the different aspects of AWS, and you won't want to miss out on these. Here, we'll tackle some of the parts of AWS that you may not know about, including web development and platforms to host which can benefit you.

Hello World LAMP Application

This is a solution stack with the four components, all of which are composed of the open-source software and it is free. This is one of the best services for you, especially if you're looking to build dynamic, capable websites to run thousands of requests all at the same time. You can use these on the EC2 instances, and from there, you can create instances within an auto-scaling group as well.

AWS Cloud9

This is an integrated development environment that lets you write, run, and debug the code that you have. It comes with a code editor, debugger, and the terminal. This also comes with Java, Python, PHP, and others, so you won't need to install files, or configure the machine to begin with this. It is cloud-based as well, so you can work on this from any internet connection machine, and you ca from there provide a seamless experience for developing the serverless applications, and it creates the perfect environment with the team. With this, you can literally code with just the browser itself. Ruby Rn the Rails Application

This is another open-source application that lets you run everything with the Ruby programming language, and you can from there, create a stack on the EC2 instance with the local MySQL database to store this. It also lets you run an Auto Scaling group with a Multi-AZ Amazon RDS database for storage, so basically, it's another good application, and if you use the Ruby programing language, this is a wonderful option.

Amazon LightSail

This is the easiest means to launch and manage any web server that utilizes AWS, and it comes with virtual machines, SSD based storage, data transfers, DNS management, and a static IP, all at a low price that is predictable. You can choose your system or application template for your website, and when your virtual private server is ready, it takes less than a minute, and you can easily manage the web server, IP address, and the DNS directly from your console. It's the perfect way to begin hosting your web server and managing as well.

Amazon Corretto

This is a multi platform production and distribution kit that works with Java, and it also includes performance enhancements and different fixes to the security in order to run thousands of different services, and it's compatible with the Java SE standard, and allows you to run these Java applications on most major systems. It is free, and supports different machines too. You can also use this for any Java distributions as well, and you get quarterly updates on this too.

Command Line Interface

This is a program for all developers, and this allows you to control multiple AWS services, and automate them with scrips. You can use this with GitHub and other devices too, and it allows you to integrate file commands as well. It work s with Linux, Windows, and Mac too in order to do command lines while on your browser.

Cloud Development Kit

Finally, we have the AWS CDK, which is a software framework that allows you to model and provision all of the application resources in programming languages that you understand. This allows you to perform actions, write scripts, maintain the templates, or learn languages specific to the domain, giving you some high-level components that preconfigure the cloud resources with the defaults being provided, so you can build these without needing to have expertise. It is great because you can use Cloud Formation, allowing you to compose and share the custom aspects of this with any requirements you may need, helping you get to new projects quite quicker.

Web development is certainly possible with AWS, and here, you learned a little bit about it.

Chapter 4 –Mobile Development services

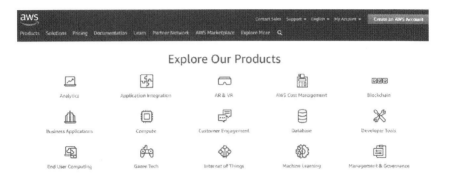

Mobile development is possible on AWS. Here, you will learn about a few of the AWS services for mobile users.

Amazon DynamoDB

This is a managed NoSQL data based and cloud service that allows for calculated and accelerated performance with scalability. It allows for you to get many volumes of data and it is very fast, and it has a very little amount of latency. This means that setting it up, configuring it, patching it, cluster scaling, and replication aren't a problem to start, and it comes with encryption. It also can scale the volumes, data, and growth without interference from the user, so if you're putting together mobile as and mobile gaming, this is great.

Amazon Cognito

This is a way for you to control and access your mobile apps, and you can authenticate these through social media apps as well, and with SAML solutions, allowing you to use your own identity system. This also lets you save local data, allowing for applications to use this even when the devices aren't online. You can even synchronize the data that users use across their app, regardless of device. You can use this to create wonderful app experiences, and you can create a scaling solution for most devices.

Amazon Pinpoint

This allows you to send messages to customers through different engagement channels, including promotional alerts and customer retention campaigns, and including but not limited to password reset and order confirmation messages as well. You can integrate this fully into both mobile and web apps, in order to capture the data and use this to figure out how you can integrate this to your apps. You can look at the messages that are delivered, clicked, or opened, and you can utilize this to figure out the messages, and you can develop audience segments and from there, you can pre-schedule the targeted campaigns via email, notifications, and campaigns that are targeted for sending educational or promotional content. You can also send out transactional messages using the Amazon Pinpoint rest API, and other transactional messages and campaigns

Device Farm

This is an app testing service that lets you work and interact with the android, iOS, and other devices at once, or reproduce those issues in real time. You can look at all of the performance data and pinpoint various issues on your app before they happen.

Appsync

This is a great one for mobile developers to securely handle all of their data both online and offline with data access, synchronization, and manipulation, and it uses a query language that's designed to build the applications by giving a flexible syntax and intuitive means for describing this, and it will help with pushing both of these together.

AWS Lambda

Finally, you have lambda, which is great for managing the servers, so you'll only pay for the computing used, and you can put codes for any apps or backend services, and you can sue this to scale the code for the best availability, and you literally can set the code up to trigger from other services within the app.

Mobile development has never been easier, and now, you can use AWS to do this for you.

Chapter 5—Code Injection Services

Amazon Athena	Amazon CloudSearch	Amazon EMR
Query data in S3 using SQL	Managed search service	Hosted Hadoop framework
Amazon Elasticsearch Service	Amazon Kinesis	Amazon Managed Streaming for Apache Kaf
Run and scale Elasticsearch clusters	Analyze real-time video and data streams	Fully managed Apache Kafka service
Amazon Redshift	Amazon QuickSight	AWS Data Pipeline
Fast, simple, cost-effective data warehousing	Fast business analytics service	Orchestration service for periodic, data-driven worl
AWS Glue	AWS Lake Formation	
Prepare and load data	Build a secure data lake in days	

AWS provides you with code injection services, and here, we'll discuss some of the best services to consider when you're trying to build an AWS data pipeline.

CodeStar

This is great for code development since it allows you to build, deploy, and utilize applications within AWS, and this in turn allows you to manage the software development activities all in one place. You can set up an entire continuous delivery tool chain within minutes, allowing you to release the code faster. It allows you to manage access, add owners, contributors, and viewers to every project, and it comes with integrated issue tracking abilities and from there, you can look at the entire software process from a dashboard and a backlog of work too quite easily.

CodeCommit

This is a fully managed source control service for repositories that are Git-based. This is great for teams to work together in order to create a secure and stable type of ecosystem, allowing you to source your own code, without scaling or infrastructure being a problem. It works with Git tools quite well, and it's perfect for giving you the right source code to the binaries necessary, and will store everything that you need. You can manage and control everything here, and create a system that everyone can use.

CodeDeploy

This is another coding system that allows you to inject code to different computing services, whether they are EC2, Lambda, Fargate, or other servers. This also comes with some new features too, which makes putting out code faster. It helps to avoid downtime during deployment of application, and it handles updating your applications automatically. This automates the software deployments too, which eliminates the error-prone operations, and from there, you can create a fully scalable service that matches the deployment needs.

CodePipeline

Finally, you've got CodePipeline which allows for a continuous delivery to help with automating the release, letting you build, test, and deploy more phases of the release process every time there's a change, based on the model you define, which lets you rapidly and reliably deliver updates and features, letting you integrate with other plugins, or even GitHub in some cases. You also only pay for the code that you utilize, so you don't have to pay any upfront fees or long-term investments.

With AWS, using their cod injection services is markedly cheaper than others, and you'll see when you use it that it's worth trying out, since there is a lot that you can utilize, and a lot of wonderful actions that you can start with.

Chapter 6—Corporate Services

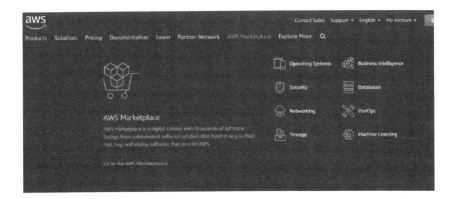

Corporations love to use AWS for different reasons, and here, we'll discuss a few of the applications that AWS has that help make running a business smoother, and easier than ever.

Business Software And Application

There is a lot of business software and application, and all of these allow for availability, flexibility, and agility, and these are all ran on the cloud with infrastructure added in order to deploy quicker, with a lower cost, and increased revenue. With AWS, using cloud computing, you'll be able to have everything on the business, and it can help run the future of your business too.

There are also Enterprise IT applications, which help with documentation, email and collaboration, and all of these help to bring about compliance requirements and security for all types of IT organizations. You can use the Microsoft active directory to look at the existing credentials, and also the multi-factor authentication, encryption support, and the ability to control and set prices for the devices, and you can even choose the region too.

Amazon Workdocs

This is literally just like Google docs, and it allows for you to have strong administration controls, and the ability for users to work together effectively. Users can comment on files, send feedback, and also upload different versions without having to utilize email, and it works on most devices. You can integrate your directories, share different things, and also control where the data is stored, and you can get 1TB of storage for 50 users for free for 390 days to see if you like this.

Alexa for Business

This is another AWS application that allows for you to get more work done. Employees can use Alexa as an assistant and it will help with making them more productive both at work, and at home. If they already use Alexa, then this can be a wonderful addition, and if they already like to use Alexa devices, this is perfect.

Amazon Workmail

This is the calendar and email service for business, for both mobile and email cloud applications, letting you go through your contacts, calendars, and client applications of choice, including Microsoft applications, and it works with IMAP protocol, or directly through a browser. It works with the existing directory and compliance requirements to help you encrypt the data and location of where it is stored. It will allow you to manage both groups, users, and resources too in order to make it possible.

Amazon Chime

Finally, you have Amazon Chime which is a service that transforms the meetings with a secure application that's trustworthy. It works across all devices so you can stay connected, suing it for online meetings, conference calls, chats, and also to share content within and outside the organization, letting you start meetings the right way.

Corporations can benefit immensely from Alexa, and these are a lot of AWS services that are offered. Here, you learned a little bit about these services, and everything about them as well.

Chapter 7—Big Data Services

Big data is a big part of AWS. Companies use this to help store large amounts of data, and here, we'll talk about some of the big data options that you can choose, that will get you the results that you need from this.

Data Lake

This is an integrate suite of different services, which allow you to manage a whole bunch of data, and build it for analytics, which allow you to handle the agility, scale, and flexibility in order to make different data types. It allows for many traditional data silos and warehouses to not be used as much, since there is a lot that you can access here, use analytics with, and other machine learning which is great without compromising security on controlling this. There are many businesses that use this too, which means that it's wonderful for those of us who want to have really secure and useful big data services.

You can move data with this, and data lakes will hold everything from gigabytes to even exabytes, and from there, you can use analytics to help analyze this, and machine learning services that work for your business.

Data movement Services

This is essentially the ability to move huge amounts of data, with the only limits being the speeds and the bandwidth used to move everything. If you want to make data transfer easy and flexible, there are many options. This allows you to move a large amount of data without needing to spend a lot.

Amazon Snowball

This is a petabyte-scale data transport system that you can use. This is one of the best for larger companies that have a lot of data to move, and it won't cost as much. You can move analytics, video libraries, image repositories, backups, to even shutdowns, and tape replacement sand application migration. It's simple, fast, and more secure than ever before. You can create a job in AWS management and the device will be shipped to you. Once this is complete, the data can be returned as well.

S3 Glacier

Storage Service [handwritten annotation]

This is a super durable, low-cost storage service that is perfect for those long-term backups for big data, since it provides comprehensive security and capabilities that fit even the most stringent of requirements. It does have an in-place functionality, which allows for powerful analytics to be there. It is definitely the cheaper option for a lot of companies that have a huge amount of data, and you can have options to access these archives too.

AWS Glue

This is a great way to extract, transform, and load all of the information, in order to provide data for analytics. You can use this to store data, allowing you to store the associated metadata, making it easily searchable, and query able, and also available for the ETL.

Amazon Redship

This is another huge data warehouse, and it's growing faster than even their top competitors, and it can handle unlimited concurrency of items as well. It is a small or large warehouse, and you can scale up to petabytes and terabytes of information, for just under a grand each year. You only pay what you need to, and you can leverage how much you spend as well, which will help you if you're worried about this. This is one of the best big data services, and the ones that even the top competitors go to.

Amazon EMR

Finally, you have this one, which is the industry-leading big data platform which allows you to process a bunch of data at almost no price, and it allows you to scale it with apache spark, hive, Hbase, Flink, and Presto, along with the scalability of EC2, and from there, you'll be able to have the elasticity to run petabyte-scale analysis for a fraction of the cost of other clusters. Developers and analysts use different notebooks for development, collaboration, and access to the data stored across different data channels in order to reduce time and operationalize analysis. Customers can use this to handle large sets of data use cases, and also look at flexible financial and scientific simulations, and also look at data transformations, and the flexibility to use on short-lived clusters that scale to meet demand, and also run available cluster using the multi-master deployment mode.

Big data is made easy with AWS, and there are many services for transferring and holding this type of data so that you're able to build a better, more useful experience, and in turn, also create a wonderful experience of you to use as well.

Chapter 8—AWS Management Services

There are also some management services to help you look at some of the different aspects of your account. Here, we'll tell you a little bit about it, and some of the other aspects of this that you need to consider when choosing this too.

AWS Identity and Access Management

This is the first means that you can use, and it allows you to create AWS users, along with groups, and also use permissions to allow, or even deny access to different resources. This is a feature of your account that's actually offered at no additional charge. This basically allows you to control who gets to see what resource, and how ti's controlled, and it also comes with a multi-factor authentication, and some username and credentials as well to make it easier.

AWS Billing and Cost management

This is a service that lets you pay the bill, monitor the usage, and it also will help with budgeting too. For newer users, this is great because you can see how much you're spending, and also look at the payment methods, and also look at the different costs that you have, and if you are someone that is using the Amazon Internet Services, they may be able to access this and pay the bill too. You can also look at the usage of your AWS account, and manage it better as well.

CloudWatch

This is a monitoring and management service that's used for system operators, site developers, engineers, and IT managers, which provides you with the data and actionable means to monitor valorous applications, respond and understand any changes in performance, optimize the resources utilized, and get a unified view of the health of your AWS account. It also monitors the operational data in the form of different logs, metrics, and other events, which gives you applications and services on this. You can also set up alarms, logs, and metrics, and also look at automated actions and issues, fixing them along the way.

AWS Managed Services

This is great for those that want to gain skills and experience. This is essentially an operating model, an on-going cost optimization and infrastructure management. You can from here implement the best practices in order to maintain the infrastructure, helping to reduce the overhead. You can change requests, monitor, patch the different areas, look at security and backup with this as well. You can literally run the infrastructure operations to direct them towards differentiation the business.

AWS management services help with building a better, more rewarding experience with AWS, and here, you learned a little bit about what that entails, and some of the key benefits of each of these too.

Chapter 9 – The Big Chapter of AWS Tips and Tricks

AWS has a wealth of information and tips and tricks that can help you with building your websites. If you've ever been curious about this, then you're in luck. In this chapter, we'll go through a wide variety of different tips and tricks that you can learn, and a lot of important details to each that'll allow you to build the best AWS protocol that you can!

Control your AWS Costs

First thing you're going to want to do is control the AWS costs, and figure out how to effectively make this less. There are a few tips that you can utilize in order to improve your AWS experience.

First and foremost, you should shutdown anything that's not being used, especially when you're done working with it. Elastic Beanstalk and AWS OpWorks allow for developers to quickly deploy and use these easily. If you do this, you'll be able to make sure that you aren't spending extra money on workloads, and you can shutdown and delete any resources not needed without problems. You can shut some of these down, and make sure that you're not spending too much.

You should also make sure that you look at th4 AWS costs and the usage. Find out where most of the expenditures are going, and if there is too much going to one place, figure out a way to reduce the usage of it. You can also use cost-management software to go deeper if you feel like you need it.

When choosing storage as well, you need to make sure that you're not spending too much on requests, whether they are PUT, HTTP, or other requests for data to transfer. For example, if you're using a standard amount of data, you should use the standard service. If you're not using a lot of data as much, put it in the infrequent-access tier, such as those that are records you may not need to use.

If you need data that needs to be retained for over 90 days, such as cold data or backups, then Glacier is the way to do it. It does take a bit longer to get some of the data retrievals, but it is a bit cheaper. Look at the different data tiers and storage, and from there, make sure you are buying only what you need.

Finally, use auto-scaling, since this will align resources with customer demand. This is great since it applies to the architecture not just in cost management, but it actually will tell you when something is unhealthy. It is incredibly easy to set up, but you'll be happy that you did it once you use this means to understand what is going on, and it can miraculously help you with your AWS business.

Launch a Linux Virtual Machine

Launching Linux virtual machine is possible with AWS, and the best way to do it, is to use Elastic Compute Cloud EC2 to do this. we'll tell you how to do it below.

The first thing that you do is of course, sign up, and from there you enter the console, and from there, you search Amazon EC2 to begin with opening this. From here, you choose to launch the instance, which in turn will help with configuring the virtual machine.

At this point, you need to configure the instance. and from there, launch it. On that screen, you'll see the Amazon Machine image, and from there, it includes the OS, and applications and servers. You can then choose the instance type, and this includes memory, CPU, networking, storage, or capacity, and you can configure this as needed for your machine. Once you've chosen, you can look at the storage, security, and tagging settings, and you can customize these as needed, but when you're learning this, do just accept the default values.

The next area is to choose an existing pair or create a new pair key, which is used to securely access your Linux instance using SSH, and from there, it's essentially Amazon stores a pair of it, which is like the lock that Amazon pairs with your key. From there, you download this, and you'll want to store it in a secure location. If you lose it, you will not be able to get access to that instance. Windows users can use this in a sub-directory, and for Mac or Linux users, just save it in a sub-directory located near the home directory. You can from there finish ad look at the instances that you have.

You can then see the column titled Instance State change from Running and the IP address that's shown, and you can refresh this by pressing the refesh button the right over the table, and you can copy the Public IP address of this, and from there, connect it to this instance, which is the next step.

Next, you connect this to an SSH, and you can install Git Bash to do this, or opening a terminal window. From there you'll want to connect to the instance, and then type in the path to the directory, and you'll typically see a response that talks about the authenticity of the host. Press enter when you see this, along with yes, and from there you should see a welcome screen, so you should have a Linux virtual machine on hat cloud. You can always terminate this by going to actions and then choosing to terminate it. It is that simple!

Deploy Code to a Virtual Machine

You can at this point deploy virtual machine code on AWS, and you do this initially by creating a key pair if you have not already. Go to management console, and then create key pair. Name this, and then choose to create this. From here, you go to the AWS management console, and then expend developer tools, and then click on code deploy console, and from there, you choose to get started, and then sample deployment, and from here, choose the next option. From here the AWS virtual machine will deploy the code on there, and from there, you can configure the instance just like before, and choose next. You can then give your application the name for it. For tutorial purposes, choose "hello world, and then go to the next step.

Next, check the location and description, making sure this is next. At this point, you will create a deployment group in the name box, and you can choose whatever you want it to be once the data is put in, and then choose next. You then are to create a service role. You can create this or you can choose to use an existing service role, and then next step. From there, you should leave the default deployment configuration on this step to help make it easy for you. Custom deployment configuration might be a bit much to begin with.

At this point, you can then choose to deploy it right now, and that's the best way to put it together. You can then deploy any application to a virtual machine, and this is really good if you have applications that work best on a virtual machine interface,

Deploy and Host a ReactJS App

This helps with determining the framework on each end, and you can use both the Git repository for this, and

Amplify for the settings of both the framework and back ended resources. You can also connect these to the amplify console in order to make it available to the content delivery network that's here. Understanding the changes to a ReactJS application will help with the deployment, and pushing it to the master branch as well.

To begin, you must confirm the environmental setup by putting node -v; into the command prompt, and you should make sure that the command returns is larger than v8.0, since if it isn't, it needs to be upgraded. At this point, you want to create a new React application, and install the package for creating react apps to begin.

If you haven't already, you should create a GitHub repository and commit the code to this. You will need the GitHub account in order to complete this. You then want to initialize and push the application to the new Github repo that is executing the commands on the interface too, so you can have it all there.

Next, you want to log into the Amplify console, which is simple. Once you've created and selected both, you start under display, and you then choose the repository service, and then choose next. You will then want to authenticate the GitHub and then return to the Amplify console, and then choose the repository that you created within the master branch earlier. From there, accept the default settings, and then choose next to continue. From there, you'll want to review the final details and choose save and deploy. At this point, the AWS amplify console will now build source code to deploy the app you can then choose the thumbnail to set up the web app in order to make it run live.

From here, you want to automatically make changes to the code, and also change the master branch of the app. Once that is complete, you choose the thumbnail on the AWS console to launch the app. Now, if you want to terminate any resources you've created, you can do it super easily with the AWS Amplify console. It will definitely help you a lot if you want to terminate resources that you are no longer using to make sure that you don't get charged. You can go to any resource that you have, choose action, and from there, choose to delete the app, and then you can confirm that you want to delete this. There you go.

Launch a WordPress Website

Launching a WordPress Website on AWS is incredibly easy with this, and it's not 3xpensive at all. It's only $3.50 a month. You can use light sail to do this, allowing you to have it on a virtual, private server with just a few clicks, and from there it can be optimized for both security and performance quite easily.

Light sail is incredibly awesome, and you can manage everything from one singular console, back everything up with snapshotting, track the metrics of the server and performance, set up domain records, access the SSH with just a click, and then add resources easily as your site grows. It is incredibly easy, and this is probably the best service to utilize.

To configure this and launch it. It's pretty easy. You first want to create an instance beforehand, and you can go to the left-hand side and choose WordPress. From there, you will get a pricing page, and you can then scroll down and click continue to begin. You can then click on the 2.2 micro on there, and then configure your instance details to load all of this. You will then need to add storage, and your tag instance, and from there, you will then set a name for this. Enter name in the box, and then WordPress in the value box. From there, you review and launch to continue this. You can from there review the configurations if you are ready to start the EC2 instance for WordPress.

At this point, you'll then want to click launch to start this. You'll then want to choose a key-pair for your instance if you're securing it via the secure shell. You can do it without it, and you'll need to make a key later on without the EC2 instance if you choose this. You then launch instances, but do be aware that this can take a few minutes. Some of these instances do require you to create a key pair, and from there, you'll need to follow that in the Linux virtual machine section if you don't know how.

At this point, you may need to look at your instances, and then choose WordPress, and you make sure that this is running. Once this is running, you can then find the public IP of the instance at the bottom, from there, you can copy the Public IP into the browser, and you should see the blog page for Hello World Appear at this instance.

You can then make changes to the website by switching back to the console management, choosing WordPress, and then clicking the actions button, then instance setting, and get system log. You'll then want to find the password, and once you have that, you can then access the WordPress Hello World page. You then add admin to the url, and press enter, and then, you enter the username and the password for the log file to continue. At this point, you should have a domain name in place for the running instance.

Register a Domain Name

If you want to use AWS, transferring the domain names to this can be a pain, but right now, the route 53 AWS service is a really good way for routing the service and the DNS for AWS materials.

Once you connect these, you can then connect it to a web app, any website running WordPress, apache, NGINX, IIS, or a website platform, and from there, you can set up a DNS for your site. It does cost a little bit to register, depending on whether you're going for a top-level domain, but if you're using a domain, you can create a hosted zone that has the same name as the domain, and you can then route the traffic to the domain for ease of access.

To begin, you go to AWS, and then choose register domain, and then enter the desired domain name, checking to see if you can get it. From there, you want to select how many years that name can be registered a domain name. You can from there select how many years you want to register that domain name. Some of the top level domain names, such as .co can be expensive. But, if can also cost more for hosting it through a server, but low-traffic sites do get free options. You'll then want to put the contact information into the next box.

You will then get sent an email to verify it, and once it's there, you then now have the documentation for registering a domain, and from there, you can set it up with AWS.

If your DNS is isn't configured you'll need to go to the domain name you entered in step two, and from there, you can choose either a static IP addressed, or a Fully Qualified

Domain Name, which is common in applications that are launched in Elastic Beanstalk or lambda, then you can choose that. From there, you can create record set button, and on the right side, you enter the www in the text box, then enter the Elastic IP address in the value box and from there, you choose to create it.

You will then need to fully verify it by typing in the new website address in the browser, and if it's there, then you're good to go!

If you don't' have a static URL, you'll need to go to the elastic IPs part of the EC2 console, and then choose to allocate new address. You can then choose VPC, and then choose Allocate. There isn't a charge for these that are connected to instances, but if you no longer run the instance, then it will cost you a tiny bit of money for it to be hosted. From there, you note the new IP address, close it, and then choose the new IP address, and then press the actions button, and choose the associate address option. From there, you should click the instance box, and then choose the option that has the instance name, and then make note of the new IP address on the column to your left. From there, you can verify it, and use it to register the domain name in the other steps.

Create and Connect to a MySQL Database

to create this environment, you first and foremost need to make sure that you're using Amazon RDS, and everything in this is started. You want to find RDS under database and then open up the Amazon RDS console. You want to make sure that you select the region to create the DB instance, and cloud resources are stored in available data center facilities, and you should choose the one that you feel fits your location.

You can then choose to create a database, and you can choose to create the engine. Choose the MySQL icon, and then choose only eligible options for the RDS free usage tier, and then next. You can then choose the different settings that works, such as storage, storage type, auto scaling, deployment, the engine version and instance class, and other features. Once finished, you can then click on the advanced features, including network and security, the public accessibility, and the zone of accessibility, and you can then choose database options that work for this too if you don't choose it.

You should go through each of these, and once finished, you can check the database instances, and you can choose what you want to do with this, whether work on creating this, and when this is changed, you connect the database to a DB instance, and you can then download the SQL client in the meantime for this. You should make sure that they're run on the same device the instance was created to allow connections only from the device which created this.

You can then download it, or not do so, and then you connect it to the SQL workbench. You go to the workbench application, then go to database, then connect to database in the menu bar, and then put the hostname, username, password, or port, which is 3306, and then choose OK. From there, you're fully connected! You can then see schema that are available, create tables, and also run queries that are there.

Store and Retrieve a File

It is pretty easy to store and retrieve the files, and to begin, you go to identity and access management, and then go to roles. Type in your identity pool name, and you can then look for the unauthenticated users, and from there, you create role policy, then policy generator, and then select, and you can then from there set up permissions in order to get actions there for a singular bucket.

From there, you add statement, then next step, and then, you can apply the policy, and from there, you should have the permissions to upload files.

from there, on the S3 console, you want to choose the file to download or open, and then you choose action, then choose download or open. If you are downloading, you specify where you want to save it, and this is the same for saving objects to the cloud, but is dependent on the OS you're using.

You can always upload files by having them file and bucket name in it. From there. You write transferUtility.Upload(and then the path.combine, and then put the environment special folder, application data, and from there, everything that you upload is put on there.

Batch upload files to the cloud

If you want to upload a batch of files, you want to use TransferManager, since this has both upload and download management on there. You can from there choose the

43

location of the files being uploaded, and the ObjectMetadata provider that will be used, allowing you to figure out where you want to store the object on the 3. Using transfer manager will help you store the files much faster, and have more files go to the location necessary.

Another option, is to do it through the AWS CLI, and from there, you choose your OS. You first want to put the windows installer in, and from there, the windows key, and then run the command box. From there, you want to add the AWS access key from the credentials.csv file you downloaded, and from there, you enter the secret access key, then the default region name, and the output format. From there, you want to create a bucket, and you can choose your fist backup bucket. One of the restrictions, is the name must be unique globally to your own personal data. If you get the option that the bucket already exists, choose something else. From there, you want to upload to the backup that's on there, and make sure that you use the syntax so that there isn't any backups or spaces. You can download this as well in the same way.

Set up a Continuous Deployment Pipeline

To do this, you'll want to make sure that you have an environment for this type of instance. You can spin together a sample environment using the AWS elastic beanstalk to host web applications without needing to launch, operate, or configure the servers. You choose PHP from the menu, and then launch now, and you can create new application in the corner, and then name it and create an environment for this. Select the PHO as a single instance environment type. If you plant to remote login for

44

this instance, choose a key pair, or otherwise default the values for the remaining options, and choose the continue deployment pipeline.

Once there, you can have a sample environment created for you to deploy the application too, in order to create an auto scaling group, S3 bucket, cloud watch alarms, and from there, a domain name for the application that you have.

You'll then get a copy of the sample code, and you do this from a source that will host the code. You can do this either via GitHub, S3, or AWS CodeCommit. Which ever one you choose, choose this, and then follow the steps for the code.

From here, you create your pipeline. You can then choose the repository, and the deployment environment. You can open up the CodePipeline console, and then create a pipeline, and you'll get an introductory page that appears to help you learn how to put together pipelines. You can then enter the name of the pipeline, and then choose next step, and you can choose the location of the source based on where you're going.

If you choose GitHub for example, you choose to connect to this, and you'll then be prompted to sign in, and then you can choose to authorize the application. You're then given a repository, and chose the forked one, and you should choose the branch that you want. Then go to the next step. The truth pipeline will require a build stage where the code is compiled and the unit trusted. CodePipeline lets you put this in, and you can build it. From there, you can then choose your beta page, and where you're beginning with this. You can choose the environment. From there, you choose the service role, and from there, allow it, and you can then create the role, and you can then return to the step f5 page, and you'll then get to see the name. You only need to create this when you build a pipeline in AWS CodePipeline.

From here, you activate and deploy the code. It will be ran automatically, and from m the source location, it'll detect the app code, and then move them to the second stage that you've got defined. It'll pass the code to elastic beanstalk, and then deploy the code in the EC2 instance. You can review the information, and then choose to create the pipeline. Once created, the pipeline will appear automatically, and you can view progress as it happens, and any failure messages as the pipeline performs this. You can further verify and monitor the progress, and it will tell you whether it will work. Once it's there, you can check the status area for the beta stage, such as AWS elastic beanstalk. You can then open up the deployment details, and choose the environment that's been created, such as the default environment, and then choose the URL that shows the website that's being deployed. That's all there is and once you're done, At this point, you'll want to clean up the resources, you'll want to delete everything that's been used, if t's a tutorial piece. To do this, you first will go to pipeline view, then edit, and then choose delete, and then choose the pipeline name and proceed to press delete. You can further terminate the elastic beanstalk application by going to the console, and then terminating. If you created an S3 to practice, always delete it so you don't et charged.

Remotely Run Commands on an EC2 Instance

The best way to remotely run commands is to first and foremost create the IAM role to begin. You'll then want to choose an instance, but this time around you should choose one that supports the instance, and from there, launch it. You should choose the Linux AMI since this is food for systems managers by default. From there, choose an instance type, and configure the details. You then nat to choose IAM role and then choose to launch this instance. You can choose a key pair and from there, configure this.

You can from here update the systems manager agent in order to automate the tasks here. You can go to services, then systems manager, and then go to managed instances, and then go to the actions menu, and from there, run command you can then put the command line to run this.

Finally, you want to run a remote shell script, by going to the run command once again, go to the document name prefix, and then type of AWS-RunShellScript, and from there, the document will upgrade the systems management, and then go to targets, and then chose the managed instance. Go down to the command parameters, and from there, type in sudo, yum, update -y and then run this, and you can check the overall status, the targets and outputs, and the instance. You want to from there go to the output on: I: XX page, and then view the output from the update command from the instance. At this point, just like before, always terminate the resources, so you're not getting charged for this.

These tips and tricks will help you with running AWS commands, and it will help you better understand how to run some of the programs and services this has to offer, which in turn will enhance the experience as well.

Conclusion

With AWS, it has never been easier to build a whole business and host a website. From hosting websites to getting domain names, to even seeing if your blog is live, it definitely is the future of businesses.

You can use this for anything from building a business with different emails that your customers can get, to even putting together vital code for running various apps that you can choose, and some of the different features of them.

The best part, is that you don't have to pay for an umbrella service which you may not use, but instead you pay as you go. If you want to have AWS host your site, then you pay for that, but it doesn't have to do everything. In fact, it very rarely will do this, and there is a lot that you can benefit from with this.

With that being said, your next step is to figure out with AWS aspects you want to consider, which ones you'll benefit from, and what you'll be able to do with each of these. Choose the best ones for your business, and the ones that you can truly benefit from, and you'll see for yourself that, there is a lot more to this than what meets the eye, and you can do a lot with AWS to benefit you, and to benefit others. So yes, use this today, and if you have any questions, don't be afraid to ask, cause it can be complicated. But, once you get used to it, AWS is pretty simple to understand, and beneficial for everyone at the end of the day, whether you're a small business, or a larger corporation that is looking to have a better, more wonderful company experience.

I hope, that you really enjoyed reading my book.

Thanks for buying the book anyway!

Made in the USA
Middletown, DE
16 May 2020